بِسْمِ اللهِ الرَّحْمٰنِ الرَّحِيْمِ

In the Name of Allah, The All-Merciful,
The Kindest towards believers.

Disclaimer

All rights reserved. No part of this publication may be reproduced, stored in a retrieval system, or transmitted in any form or by any means, electronic, mechanical, photocopying, recording, or otherwise, without the prior written permission of the publisher, except in the case of brief quotations quoted in articles or reviews.

Contact : Admin@islamiclessonsmadeeasy.com.au

Visit us :
Facebook.com/islamiclessonsmadeeasy
Youtube.com/islamiclessonsmadeeasy
Instagram.com/islamic_lessons_me
Islamiclessonsmadeeasy.com.au
Ilme.net.au

The pictures used are the property of Islamic Lessons Made Easy. The content and rulings are taken from various leading scholars and are presented in a simplified manner. Therefore, for the exact definition and explanation, please refer to the original sources.

First Edition
©Copyright 2025 Islamic Lessons Made Easy

Contents

Transliteration	4
Introduction	5
Etiquettes of Qurān	6
Sūrah al-Masad	8
Summary	24
Glossary	28

Transliteration

ا	a	ق	q
ب	b	ك	k
ت	t	ل	l
ث	th	م	m
ج	j	ن	n
ح	ḥ	ه	h
خ	kh	و	w
د	d	ي	y
ذ	dh	ئ / آ / ـا	ā
ر	r	ـِي	ī
ز	z	ـُو	ū
س	s		
ش	sh		
ص	ṣ		
ض	ḍ		
ط	ṭ		
ظ	ẓ		
ع	ʿ		
غ	gh		
ف	f		

ء	Read with a sudden pause of air.
ﷺ	Blessings of Allah be upon him and his family.
عليها السلام	Peace be upon her.
عليه السلام	Peace be upon him.
سبحانه وتعالى	Glorious and Exalted Is He.

Introduction

Tafsīr is an Arabic word that means 'explanation'; it helps us understand what the verses of the Qurān really mean. Scholars study the Qurān by looking at its language, the history behind the verses and other aspects. They also think about how the verses were revealed and how we can use these teachings in our daily lives.

Tafsīr helps us connect with our faith and learn how to use the lessons of the Qurān today. It makes the wisdom of the Qurān easier to understand and more useful for us.

When we made this *Tafsīr*, we worked hard to gather ideas from trusted scholars and important books. We wanted to explain the Qurān in a way that is easy for you to understand.

We hope this *Tafsīr* helps you on your journey to learn more about the Qurān and your faith.

Etiquettes of Qurān

Before reciting, it is recommended to say:

أَعُوذُ بِاللَّهِ مِنَ الشَّيْطَانِ الرَّجِيمِ

A'ūdhu billāhi minash shayṭānir rajīm

I seek refuge with Allah from the accursed devil.

Then say:

بِسْمِ اللَّهِ الرَّحْمَٰنِ الرَّحِيمِ

Bismillāhir Raḥmānir Raḥīm

In the name of Allah, The Most Gracious, The Most Merciful.

- Make sure you have performed Wuḍū before touching any verse of the Qurān
- When reading the Qurān, it is better to face the Qiblah
- Make sure that the place where the Qurān is read is free from impurities
- Don't put the Qurān on the ground or anywhere it might get dirty
- Don't place anything on top of the Qurān
- When you recite the Qurān, try to pronounce the words correctly
- Take time to reflect on what the verses mean

After finishing your recitation, say:

صَدَقَ اللهُ العَلِيُّ العَظِيمُ

Ṣadaq Allāhul 'Aliyyul 'Aẓīm

Allah, the Sublime, the Great, has spoken the truth.

Sūrah al-Masad

Sūrah al-Masad

Sūrah al-Masad is the 111th chapter of the Qurān.

It talks about a man named Abū Lahab, who was the uncle of Prophet Muhammad ﷺ. Even though he was a family member, he did not support the Prophet ﷺ and tried to stop him from spreading Islam.

He and his wife made life very hard for the Prophet ﷺ, and this *Sūrah* tells us that because of their bad actions, they will face punishment.

When Allah ﷻ told the Prophet ﷺ to start inviting people to Islam, the Prophet ﷺ climbed a mountain in Mecca and called everyone to gather.

Once the people arrived, he asked them:
"If I told you that an army was coming from behind this mountain, would you believe me?"

"Yes, we would believe you because you always tell the truth", the people replied.

Then the Prophet ﷺ said:

"I am a messenger from Allah ﷻ, warning you to stop worshipping idols and to believe in the One True God."

Abū Lahab, who was in the crowd, got very angry and shouted, "May you be ruined! Is this why you called us here?"

Because of Abū Lahab's rude behavior, Allah ﷻ revealed Sūrah al-Masad, showing the consequences of his disrespectful words and behaviour towards the Prophet ﷺ.

The Holy Prophet ﷺ :

I hope for the one who recites Sūrah al-Masad that God does not place him and Abū Lahab in the same place [in the Hereafter].

(Majmaʿ al-Bayān)

بِسْمِ اللَّهِ الرَّحْمَٰنِ الرَّحِيمِ

Bismillāhir Raḥmānir Raḥīm

In the Name of Allah, The Most Gracious,
The Most Merciful.

تَبَّتْ يَدَا أَبِي لَهَبٍ وَتَبَّ

Tabbat yadā abī lahabin watabb

May Abū Lahab and his hands be destroyed.

The words *tabbat* (تَبَّت) and *watabb* (وَتَبَّ) describe a deep loss that leads to total destruction.

This describes what happened to Abū Lahab perfectly because he died from a terrible disease. His body smelled so awful that people avoided it for days.

The word *yadā* (يَدَ - hands) could refer to the physical hands that Abū Lahab used to harm the Prophet ﷺ. These hands, which were once used to show his aggression, will also face destruction.

Another interpretation is that the word *yadā* represents all of Abū Lahab's actions—everything he did in opposition to Islam and the Prophet ﷺ—will ultimately be destroyed and of no benefit.

مَآ أَغْنَىٰ عَنْهُ مَالُهُۥ وَمَا كَسَبَ

Mā aghnā ʿanhu māluhū wamā kasab

His wealth and everything he has
will not help him.

Abū Lahab was a rich and arrogant person who thought his money, status and children would protect and benefit him.

However, Allah ﷻ makes it clear that none of these things will save him from the punishment.

This shows us that no amount of money or power can protect someone from the punishment of Allah ﷻ.

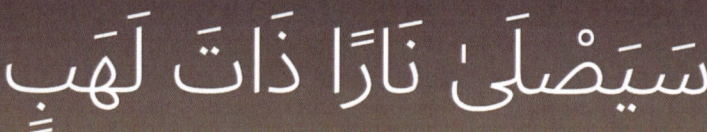

Sayaṣlā nāran dhāta lahab

Very soon he will burn in a flaming fire.

The word *nār* (نَار) means fire, and *lahab* (لَهَب) refers to a flame. Together, they describe a blazing, scorching fire that is very intense.

This verse is saying that Abū Lahab will be thrown into this fierce and blazing fire in the Hereafter because of his actions and disbelief.

وَامْرَأَتُهُۥ حَمَّالَةَ الْحَطَبِ

Wamra-atuhū ḥammālatal ḥaṭab

And his wife (will also burn in the flaming fire), carrying firewood.

Firewood fuels a fire, and with her actions, the wife of Abū Lahab fueled the fire of Hell for herself.

Some have said that this refers to how she used to carry thorny branches and place them in the path of the Prophet ﷺ to harm him. As a result, her punishment is described as fueling her own place in Hell.

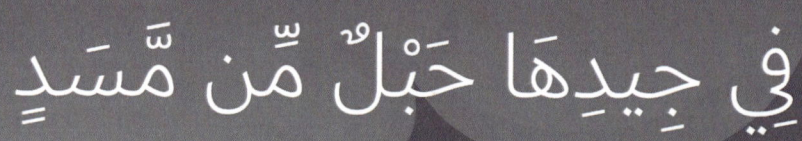

فِي جِيدِهَا حَبْلٌ مِّن مَّسَدٍ

fī jīdihā ḥablum mim masad

Around her neck will be a rope of palm fibre.

The word *masad* (مَسَد) refers to a rope made of palm fibers.

Some have said that this rope will be extremely rough, tight, heavy and unbearably hot, making it impossible for her to remove it from around her neck. This symbolises her severe punishment.

Others have explained that Abū Lahab's wife once owned a valuable necklace, and she swore to sell it and use the money to harm the Prophet ﷺ. In response, Allah ﷻ punished her with such a punishment.

Summary

Sūrah al-Masad is a short chapter that highlights the consequences of opposing the truth.

It specifically condemns Abū Lahab and his wife for their hostility towards the Prophet ﷺ and their efforts to harm him and his mission.

This *Sūrah* shows that no amount of money or status can protect someone from the punishment of Allah ﷻ if they reject the truth. Even being closely related to the Prophet ﷺ, as Abū Lahab was, did not protect him from punishment due to his actions.

The Sūrah serves as a warning against arrogance, hatred towards the truth and the dangers of opposing the guidance of Allah ﷻ.

Glossary

Lahab	- Blazing fire
Masad	- Palm Fibre
Nār	- Fire
Qiblah	- Direction of the Ka'bah
Sūrah	- Chapter
Sūrah al-Masad	- Chapter of the Palm Fibre
Tabbat	- Destruction
Yadā	- Hands

Credit

All praise belongs to Allah, the All Merciful towards all existents, the Kindest towards believers. He Who has given us enough patience and courage to complete this book.

Islamic Lessons Made Easy would like to thank all those involved in this project for their hard work and commitment.

CREATOR	EDITORS
Abbas Ibrahim	Kawthar Ibrahim
	Sheikh Dr Zaid Alsalami

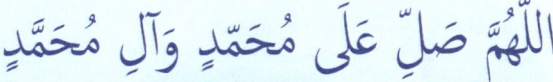

Allahumma ṣalli 'ala Muḥammadi(n)w wa āli Muḥammad
O Allah, (please do) bless Muḥammad and the Household of Muḥammad

Contact: admin@islamiclessonsmadeeasy.com.au

Visit us:
Facebook.com/islamiclessonsmadeeasy
Youtube.com/islamiclessonsmadeeasy
Instagram.com/islamic_lessons_me
Islamiclessonsmadeeasy.com.au
Ilme.net.au

www.ingramcontent.com/pod-product-compliance
Lightning Source LLC
Chambersburg PA
CBRC091202070526
44583CB00008B/183